THE BEST OF BO

A Medley Including THE JAMES BOND THEME,
YOU ONLY LIVE TWICE, LIVE AND LET DIE, FOR
and DIAMONDS ARE FOREVER

SATB, accompanied, with optional guitar, bass and drums

See page 31 for credits.
Arranged by NED GINSBURG

* Guitar: Play ad lib. from chord symbols in piano part.
  Bass: Play bottom notes in left hand of piano part, adjusting octaves as necessary.
** Guitar: Solo, "picked" sound, sounding octave lower (on low E string).

See page 31 for copyright information.

CO295C1X

* If performing without staging, play as written both times. This section is played 15 times on the Accompaniment cassette.

16

Hand claps:

end claps

119 (Regular feel)

unis. *f*

What does it mat-ter to ya, when you got a job to do— you got-ta

unis. *f*

unis.

119 (Regular feel)

A♭9

E♭7

do it *right.— You got-ta give the oth-er guy a fight!———

B♭9

Cm

D♭

* Original text: . . . do it well. You gotta give the other fellow hell!

CO295C1X

"For Your Eyes Only"

your eyes on-ly can see me through the night.   For

your eyes on-ly I nev-er need to hide.

You can see so much in me,— so much in me that's new.   I

24

26

DRUMS